Summary

In 2002, the International Atomic Energy Agency (IAEA) began investigating allegations that Iran had conducted clandestine nuclear activities. Ultimately, the agency reported that some of these activities had violated Tehran's IAEA safeguards agreement. The IAEA has not stated definitively that Iran has pursued nuclear weapons, but has also not yet been able to conclude that the country's nuclear program is exclusively for peaceful purposes. The IAEA Board of Governors referred the matter to the U.N. Security Council in February 2006. Since then, the council has adopted six resolutions, the most recent of which (Resolution 1929) was adopted in June 2010.

The Security Council has required Iran to cooperate fully with the IAEA's investigation of its nuclear activities, suspend its uranium enrichment program, suspend its construction of a heavy-water reactor and related projects, and ratify the Additional Protocol to its IAEA safeguards agreement. However, a November 2011 report from IAEA Director-General Yukiya Amano to the agency's Board of Governors indicated that Tehran has continued to defy the council's demands by continuing work on its uranium enrichment program and heavy-water reactor program. Iran has signed, but not ratified, its Additional Protocol.

Iran and the IAEA agreed in August 2007 on a work plan to clarify the outstanding questions regarding Tehran's nuclear program. Most of these questions have essentially been resolved, but then-IAEA Director-General Mohamed ElBaradei told the agency's board in June 2008 that the agency still has questions regarding "possible military dimensions to Iran's nuclear programme." The IAEA has reported for some time that it has not been able to make progress on these matters.

This report provides a brief overview of Iran's nuclear program and describes the legal basis for the actions taken by the IAEA board and the Security Council. It will be updated as events warrant.

Contents

Appendixes

Contacts

Introduction

Iran ratified the nuclear Nonproliferation Treaty (NPT) in 1970. Article III of the treaty requires non-nuclear-weapon states-parties[1] to accept comprehensive International Atomic Energy Agency (IAEA) safeguards; Tehran concluded a comprehensive safeguards agreement with the IAEA in 1974.[2] In 2002, the agency began investigating allegations that Iran had conducted clandestine nuclear activities; the IAEA ultimately reported that some of these activities had violated Tehran's safeguards agreement. The agency has not stated definitively that Iran has pursued nuclear weapons, but has also not yet been able to conclude that the country's nuclear program is exclusively for peaceful purposes. The IAEA continues to investigate the program.

Following more than three years of investigation, the IAEA Board of Governors referred the matter to the U.N. Security Council in February 2006. Since then, the council has adopted six resolutions requiring Iran to take steps to alleviate international concerns about its nuclear program. This report provides a brief overview of Iran's nuclear program and describes the legal basis for the actions taken by the IAEA board and the Security Council.

For more detailed information about Iran's nuclear program, see CRS Report RL34544, *Iran's Nuclear Program: Status*, by Paul K. Kerr. For more information about the state of international diplomacy with Iran, see CRS Report RL32048, *Iran: U.S. Concerns and Policy Responses*, by Kenneth Katzman.

Background

Iran's construction of a gas centrifuge-based uranium enrichment facility is currently the main source of proliferation concern. Gas centrifuges enrich uranium by spinning uranium hexafluoride gas at high speeds to increase the concentration of the uranium-235 isotope. Such centrifuges can produce both low-enriched uranium (LEU), which can be used in nuclear power reactors, and highly enriched uranium (HEU), which is one of the two types of fissile material used in nuclear weapons. HEU can also be used as fuel in certain types of nuclear reactors. Iran also has a uranium-conversion facility, which converts uranium oxide into several compounds, including uranium hexafluoride. Tehran claims that it wants to produce LEU for its current and future power reactors.

Iran's construction of a reactor moderated by heavy water has also been a source of concern. Although Tehran says that the reactor, which Iran is building at Arak, is intended for the production of medical isotopes, it is a proliferation concern because the reactor's spent fuel will contain plutonium well-suited for use in nuclear weapons. In order to be used in nuclear weapons, however, plutonium must be separated from the spent fuel—a procedure called "reprocessing." Iran has said that it will not engage in reprocessing.

---

[1] The NPT defines a nuclear-weapon state as "one which has manufactured and exploded a nuclear weapon or other nuclear explosive device" prior to January 1, 1967. These states are China, France, Russia, the United Kingdom, and the United States.

[2] INFCIRC/214, available at http://www.iaea.org/Publications/Documents/Infcircs/Others/infcirc214.pdf.

Iran and the IAEA agreed in August 2007 on a work plan to clarify the outstanding questions regarding Tehran's nuclear program.[3] Most of these questions, which had contributed to suspicions that Iran had been pursuing a nuclear weapons program, have essentially been resolved. Then-IAEA Director-General Mohamed ElBaradei, however, told the IAEA board June 2, 2008, that there is "one remaining major [unresolved] issue," which concerns questions regarding "possible military dimensions to Iran's nuclear programme." A November 8, 2011, report[4] from IAEA Director-General Yukiya Amano to the Security Council and the IAEA board indicates that the agency has not made any substantive progress on these matters. Tehran has questioned the authenticity of some of the evidence underlying the agency's concerns and maintains that it has not done any work on nuclear weapons.

Iran has also expressed concern to the IAEA that resolving some of these issues would require agency inspectors to have "access to sensitive information related to its conventional military and missile related activities." The IAEA, according to a September 2008 report from ElBaradei, has stated its willingness to discuss with Iran

> modalities that could enable Iran to demonstrate credibly that the activities referred to in the documentation are not nuclear related, as Iran asserts, while protecting sensitive information related to its conventional military activities.[5]

Indeed, the agency says that it has made several specific proposals, but Tehran has not yet provided the requested information.

Several UN Security Council Resolutions, the most recent of which (Resolution 1929) was adopted June 9, 2010, require Iran to cooperate fully with the IAEA's investigation of its nuclear activities, suspend its uranium enrichment program, suspend its construction of a heavy-water reactor and related projects, and ratify the Additional Protocol to its IAEA safeguards agreement.[6] Resolution 1929 also requires Tehran to refrain from "any activity related to ballistic missiles capable of delivering nuclear weapons." However, Amano's November 2011 report indicated that Tehran has continued to defy the council's demands by continuing work on its uranium enrichment program and heavy-water reactor program. Iranian officials have repeatedly stated that Iran will not suspend its enrichment program. Tehran has signed, but not ratified, its Additional Protocol. Iran has also continued its extensive ballistic missile program.[7] Resolution 1929 also requires Iran to comply with the modified Code 3.1 of its subsidiary arrangement, but Iran has not yet done so.[8]

---

[3] The text is available at http://www.iaea.org/Publications/Documents/Infcircs/2007/infcirc711.pdf.

[4] GOV/2011/65, available at http://www.iaea.org/Publications/Documents/Board/2011/gov2011-69.pdf.

[5] GOV/2008/38, available at http://www.iaea.org/Publications/Documents/Board/2008/gov2008-38.pdf.

[6] Iran is also constructing a plant for the production of heavy water.

[7] See CRS Report RS22758, *Iran's Ballistic Missile Programs: An Overview*, by Steven A. Hildreth.

[8] See "Potential Noncompliance Since September 2005."

Iran and the IAEA

As noted, Iran is a party to the NPT and has concluded a comprehensive safeguards agreement. Such agreements are designed to enable the IAEA to detect the diversion of nuclear material from peaceful purposes to nuclear weapons uses, as well as to detect undeclared nuclear activities and material.[9] Safeguards include agency inspections and monitoring of declared nuclear facilities. Although comprehensive safeguards agreements give the IAEA the authority "to verify the absence of undeclared nuclear material and activities, the tools available to it to do so, under such agreements, are limited," according to the agency.[10]

As a practical matter, the IAEA's ability to inspect and monitor nuclear facilities in a particular country pursuant to that government's comprehensive safeguards agreements is limited to facilities that have been declared by the government.[11] Additional Protocols to IAEA comprehensive safeguards agreements increase the agency's ability to investigate undeclared nuclear facilities and activities by increasing the IAEA's authority to inspect certain nuclear-related facilities and demand information from member states.[12] Iran signed such a protocol in December 2003 and agreed to implement the agreement pending ratification. Tehran stopped adhering to its Additional Protocol in 2006.

The IAEA's authority to investigate nuclear-weapons-related activity is limited. Then-IAEA Director-General ElBaradei explained in a 2005 interview that "we don't have an all-encompassing mandate to look for every computer study on weaponization. Our mandate is to make sure that all nuclear materials in a country are declared to us."[13] Similarly, a February 2006 report from ElBaradei to the IAEA board stated that "absent some nexus to nuclear material the Agency's legal authority to pursue the verification of possible nuclear weapons related activity is limited."[14]

The current public controversy over Iran's nuclear program began in August 2002, when the National Council of Resistance on Iran (NCRI), an Iranian exile group, revealed information during a press conference (some of which later proved to be accurate) that Tehran had built nuclear-related facilities that it had not revealed to the IAEA. The United States had been aware of at least some of these activities, according to knowledgeable former officials.[15] Prior to the NCRI's revelations, the IAEA had expressed concerns that Iran had not been providing the agency with all relevant information about its nuclear programs, but had never found the country in violation of its safeguards agreement.

---

[9] *IAEA Safeguards Glossary.* Comprehensive safeguards agreements are based on a model described in INFCIRC 153, available at http://www.iaea.org/Publications/Documents/Infcircs/Others/infcirc153.pdf.

[10] *The Safeguards System of the International Atomic Energy Agency.* Available at http://www.iaea.org/OurWork/SG/documents/safeg_system.pdf.

[11] *IAEA Safeguards Glossary.*

[12] Additional Protocols for an individual IAEA member state are based on the agency's Model Additional Protocol (INFCIRC/540), available at http://www.iaea.org/Publications/Documents/Infcircs/1997/infcirc540c.pdf.

[13] "Tackling the Nuclear Dilemma: An Interview with IAEA Director-General Mohamed ElBaradei," February 4, 2005, available at http://www.armscontrol.org/act/2005_03/ElBaradei.

[14] GOV/2006/15, available at http://www.iaea.org/Publications/Documents/Board/2006/gov2006-15.pdf.

[15] Gary Samore, Former Senior Director for Nonproliferation and Export Controls on the National Security Council, personal communication June 5, 2008; Director of Central Intelligence George J. Tenet, "DCI Remarks on Iraq's WMD Programs," February 5, 2004, available at https://www.cia.gov/news-information/speeches-testimony/2004/tenet_georgetownspeech_02052004.html.

In fall 2002, the IAEA began to investigate Iran's nuclear activities at the sites named by the NCRI; inspectors visited the sites the following February. Adopting its first resolution (GOV/2003/69)[16] on the matter in September 2003, the IAEA board called on Tehran to increase its cooperation with the agency's investigation, suspend its uranium enrichment activities, and "unconditionally sign, ratify and fully implement" an Additional Protocol.

In October 2003, Iran concluded a voluntary agreement with France, Germany, and the United Kingdom, collectively known as the "E3," to suspend its enrichment activities, sign and implement an Additional Protocol to its IAEA safeguards agreement, and comply fully with the IAEA's investigation.[17] As a result, the agency's board decided to refrain from referring the matter to the U.N. Security Council. As noted, Tehran signed this Additional Protocol in December 2003, but has never ratified it.

Ultimately, the IAEA's investigation, as well as information Iran provided after the October 2003 agreement, revealed that Iran had engaged in a variety of clandestine nuclear-related activities, some of which violated the country's safeguards agreement (see **Appendix A**). After October 2003, Iran continued some of its enrichment-related activities, but Tehran and the E3 agreed in November 2004 to a more detailed suspension agreement.[18] However, Iran resumed uranium conversion in August 2005 under the leadership of President Mahmoud Ahmadinejad, who had been elected two months earlier.

On September 24, 2005, the IAEA Board of Governors adopted a resolution (GOV/2005/77)[19] that, for the first time, found Iran to be in noncompliance with its IAEA safeguards agreement. The board, however, did not refer Iran to the Security Council, choosing instead to give Tehran additional time to comply with the board's demands. The resolution urged Iran

- to implement transparency measures including access to individuals, documentation relating to procurement, dual use equipment, certain military owned workshops and research and development locations;

- to re-establish full and sustained suspension of all enrichment-related activity;

- to reconsider the construction of the research reactor moderated by heavy water;

- to ratify promptly and implement in full the Additional Protocol; and

- to continue to act in accordance with the provisions of the Additional Protocol.

No international legal obligations required Tehran to take these steps. But ElBaradei's September 2008 report asserted that, without Iranian implementation of such "transparency measures," the IAEA "will not be in a position to progress in its verification of the absence of undeclared nuclear material and activities in Iran."

Iran announced in January 2006 that it would resume research and development on its centrifuges at Natanz. The next month, the IAEA Board of Governors referred Iran's case to the UN Security

---

[16] Available at http://www.iaea.org/Publications/Documents/Board/2003/gov2003-69.pdf.

[17] The text of the agreement is available at http://www.iaea.org/NewsCenter/Focus/IaeaIran/ statement_iran21102003.shtml.

[18] The text of the agreement is available at http://www.iaea.org/Publications/Documents/Infcircs/2004/infcirc637.pdf.

[19] Available at http://www.iaea.org/Publications/Documents/Board/2005/gov2005-77.pdf.

Council.[20] Tehran announced shortly after that it would stop implementing its Additional Protocol. (For details, see "Iran and the U.N. Security Council" below.)

Potential Noncompliance Since September 2005

Iran further scaled back its cooperation with the IAEA in March 2007, when the government told the agency that it would stop complying with a portion of the subsidiary arrangements for its IAEA safeguards agreement.[21] That provision, to which Iran agreed in 2003, requires Tehran to provide design information for new nuclear facilities "as soon as the decision to construct, or to authorize construction, of such a facility has been taken, whichever is earlier." Since March 2007, Iran has argued that it is only obligated to adhere to the previous notification provisions of its subsidiary arrangements, which required Tehran to provide design information for a new facility 180 days before introducing nuclear material into it.[22]

This decision has constituted the basis of Iran's stated rationale for its refusal to provide the IAEA with some information concerning its nuclear program. For example, Tehran has refused to provide updated design information for the heavy-water reactor under construction at Arak. Similarly, Tehran had refused to provide the IAEA with design information for a reactor that Iran intends to construct at Darkhovin. Although Iran provided the agency with preliminary design information in a September 22, 2009, letter, the IAEA has requested Tehran to "provide additional clarifications" of the information, according to a November 2009 report.[23] Amano reported in September 2010 that Iran has "has provided only limited design information with respect to" the reactor.[24] Iran has also argued, based on its March 2007 decision, that its failure to notify the IAEA before September 2009 that it has been constructing a gas-centrifuge uranium enrichment facility, called the Fordow facility, near the city of Qom is consistent with Tehran's safeguards obligations. Exactly when Iran decided to construct the facility is unclear. Amano reported in November 2011 that the IAEA has requested information from Iran regarding the Fordow construction decision, but Tehran has not yet responded to all of the agency's requests.

Both the 2007 decision, which the IAEA has asked Iran to "reconsider," and Tehran's refusal to provide the design information appear to be inconsistent with the government's safeguards obligations. Although Article 39 of Iran's safeguards agreement states that the subsidiary arrangements "may be extended or changed by agreement between" Iran and the IAEA, the agreement does not provide for a unilateral modification or suspension of any portion of those arrangements.[25][26] Moreover, the IAEA legal adviser explained in a March 2009 statement that

---

[20] For details on the IAEA's authority to refer noncompliance cases to the Security Council, see "Iran and the U.N. Security Council."

[21] According to the 2001 IAEA Safeguards Glossary, subsidiary arrangements describe the "technical and administrative procedures for specifying how the provisions laid down in a safeguards agreement are to be applied."

[22] During a November 2011 session of the Non-Aligned Movement, Ambassador Ali Asghar Soltanieh, Iran's Permanent Representative to the IAEA, characterized the modified Code 3.1 as "merely a suggestion" by the IAEA Board of Governors. See "Iran Provides 20 Answers to Clarify Ambiguities about Its Nuclear Program," *Tehran Times*, November 9,2011. Available at http://www.tehrantimes.com/politics/4362-iran-provides-20-answers-to-clarify-ambiguities-about-its-nuclear-program.

[23] GOV/2009/74, available at http://isis-online.org/uploads/isis-reports/documents/IAEA_Report_Iran_16November2009pdf_1.pdf.

[24] GOV/2010/46.

[25] See also GOV/2007/22, available at http://www.iaea.org/Publications/Documents/Board/2007/gov2007-22.pdf. Security Council Resolution 1929 affirmed that Code 3.1 "cannot be modified nor suspended unilaterally."

Tehran's failure to provide design information for the reactors is "inconsistent with" Iran's obligations under its subsidiary arrangements. The adviser, however, added that "it is difficult to conclude that" Tehran's refusal to provide the information "in itself constitutes non-compliance with, or a breach of" Iran's safeguards agreement. Nevertheless, a November 2009 report from ElBaradei described Tehran's failures both to notify the agency of the decision to begin constructing the Fordow facility, as well as to provide the relevant design information in a timely fashion, as "inconsistent with" Iran's safeguards obligations. The report similarly described Iran's delay in providing design information for the Darkhovin reactor.

Amano's November 2011 report also requested that Tehran provide the IAEA with information regarding any decisions to construct new facilities. Iran has announced that it intends to build additional enrichment facilities, although subsequent Iranian statements suggest that these facilities may not be built in the short term.[27] The IAEA has also requested that Iran provide information concerning a February 2010 Iranian announcement that it "possessed laser enrichment technology," and Iranian statements that the government is planning to construct new uranium enrichment facilities and is designing a nuclear reactor similar to a research reactor located in Tehran. Iran may have violated its safeguards agreement if it has made decisions to construct new enrichment facilities without informing the IAEA.

Iran's March 2007 decision also formed the basis for Tehran's refusal until August 2009 to allow IAEA inspectors to verify design information for the Arak reactor. This action also appeared to be inconsistent with Tehran's safeguards agreement. Article 48 of that agreement states that the IAEA "may send inspectors to facilities to verify the design information provided to the Agency"; in fact, the agency has a "continuing right" to do so, according to a November 2008 report from ElBaradei.[28] Moreover, the legal adviser's statement characterized Iran's ongoing refusal to allow IAEA inspectors to verify the Arak reactor's design information as "inconsistent with" Tehran's obligations under its safeguards agreement.[29] IAEA inspectors visited the reactor facility in August 2009 to verify design information, according to a report ElBaradei issued the same month.[30] Inspectors have visited the facility several more times, according to several reports from Amano.

In addition to the lapses described above, Iran's failure to notify the IAEA of its decision to enrich uranium to a maximum of 20% uranium-235 in time for agency inspectors to adjust their safeguards procedures may, according to a February 2010 report from Amano, have violated Iran's IAEA safeguards agreement.[31] Article 45 of that agreement requires that Tehran notify the IAEA "with design information in respect of a modification relevant for safeguards purposes sufficiently in advance for the safeguards procedures to be adjusted when necessary," according to Amano's report, which describes Iran's enrichment decision as "clearly relevant for safeguards purposes."

(...continued)

[26] Available at http://www.armscontrolwonk.com/file_download/162/Legal_Adviser_Iran.pdf.

[27] See CRS Report RL34544, *Iran's Nuclear Program: Status*, by Paul K. Kerr.

[28] GOV/2008/59. Security Council Resolution 1929 affirmed this statement.

[29] Iran stated in an April 2007 letter to the IAEA that, given Tehran's March 2007 decision regarding the subsidiary arrangements to its safeguards agreement, such visits were unjustified.

[30] GOV/2009/55, available at http://www.iaea.org/Publications/Documents/Board/2009/gov2009-55.pdf.

[31] GOV/2010/10, available at http://www.pdfdownload.org/pdf2html/view_online.php?url= http%3A%2F%2Fwww.iaea.org%2FPublications%2FDocuments%2FBoard%2F2010%2Fgov2010-10.pdf.

The IAEA board has neither formally found that any of the Iranian actions described above are in noncompliance with Tehran's safeguards agreement, nor referred these issues to the U.N. Security Council. The IAEA board adopted a resolution November 27, 2009, that described Iran's failure to notify the agency of the Fordow facility as "inconsistent with" the subsidiary arrangements under Iran's safeguards agreement, but this statement did not constitute a formal finding of noncompliance. A November 18, 2011, IAEA board resolution expressed "serious concern" that Tehran has not complied with the obligations described in IAEA Board of Governors and U.N. Security Council resolutions, but the November resolution did not contain a formal finding of noncompliance.

Iran and the U.N. Security Council

As noted, Iran announced in January 2006 that it would resume research and development on its centrifuges at Natanz. In response, the IAEA board adopted a resolution (GOV/2006/14)[32] February 4, 2006, referring the matter to the Security Council and reiterating its call for Iran to take the measures specified in the September resolution. Two days later, Tehran announced that it would stop implementing its Additional Protocol.

On March 29, 2006, the U.N. Security Council President issued a statement, which was not legally binding, that called on Iran to "take the steps required" by the February IAEA board resolution. The council subsequently adopted six resolutions concerning Iran's nuclear program: 1696 (July 2006), 1737 (December 2006), 1747 (March 2007), 1803 (March 2008), 1835 (September 2008), and 1929 (June 2010). The second, third, fourth, and sixth resolutions imposed a variety of restrictions on Iran.

Resolution 1696 was the first to place legally-binding Security Council requirements on Iran with respect to its nuclear program. That resolution made mandatory the IAEA-demanded suspension and called on Tehran to implement the transparency measures called for by the IAEA board's February 2006 resolution. Resolution 1737 reiterated these requirements but expanded the suspension's scope to include "work on all heavy water-related projects." It is worth noting that the Security Council has acknowledged (in Resolution 1803, for example) Iran's rights under Article IV of the NPT, which states that parties to the treaty have "the inalienable right ... to develop research, production and use of nuclear energy for peaceful Purposes."[33]

As noted, Resolution 1929 also requires Tehran to refrain from "any activity related to ballistic missiles capable of delivering nuclear weapons" and to comply with the modified Code 3.1 of its subsidiary arrangement.

---

[32] Available at http://www.iaea.org/Publications/Documents/Board/2006/gov2006-14.pdf.

[33] The treaty text is available at http://www.iaea.org/Publications/Documents/Infcircs/Others/infcirc140.pdf.

Authority for IAEA and U.N. Security Council Actions

The legal authority for the actions taken by the IAEA Board of Governors and the U.N. Security Council is found in both the IAEA Statute and the U.N. Charter. The following sections discuss the relevant portions of those documents.

IAEA Statute[34]

Two sections of the IAEA Statute explain what the agency should do if an IAEA member state is found to be in noncompliance with its safeguards agreement.[35] Article III B. 4. of the statute states that the IAEA is to submit annual reports to the U.N. General Assembly and, "when appropriate," to the U.N. Security Council. If "there should arise questions that are within the competence of the Security Council," the article adds, the IAEA "shall notify the Security Council, as the organ bearing the main responsibility for the maintenance of international peace and security."

Additionally, Article XII C. states that IAEA inspectors are to report non-compliance issues to the agency's Director-General, who is to report the matter to the IAEA Board of Governors. The board is then to "call upon the recipient State or States to remedy forthwith any non-compliance which it finds to have occurred," as well as "report the non-compliance to all members and to the Security Council and General Assembly of the United Nations."

In the case of Iran, the September 24, 2005, IAEA board resolution (GOV/2005/77) stated that the board

> found that Iran's many failures and breaches of its obligations to comply with its NPT Safeguards Agreement, as detailed in GOV/2003/75 [a November 2003 report from ElBaradei], constitute non compliance in the context of Article XII.C of the Agency's Statute;

According to the resolution, the board also found

> that the history of concealment of Iran's nuclear activities referred to in the Director General's report [GOV/2003/75], the nature of these activities, issues brought to light in the course of the Agency's verification of declarations made by Iran since September 2002 and the resulting absence of confidence that Iran's nuclear programme is exclusively for peaceful purposes have given rise to questions that are within the competence of the Security Council, as the organ bearing the main responsibility for the maintenance of international peace and security.

ElBaradei issued the report cited by the resolution, GOV/2003/75, in November 2003.[36] It described a variety of Iranian nuclear activities, which are detailed in **Appendix A**, that violated Tehran's safeguards agreement. ElBaradei subsequently reported that Iran has taken corrective

---

[34] The IAEA Statute is not self-executing; the Agency implements safeguards agreements reached with individual governments. As noted, comprehensive safeguards agreements are based on a model described in INFCIRC 153.

[35] The text of the IAEA Statute is available at http://www.iaea.org/About/statute_text html.

[36] Available at http://www.iaea.org/Publications/Documents/Board/2003/gov2003-75.pdf.

measures to address these safeguards breaches. As noted above, the 2005 resolution called on Iran to take a variety of actions that Tehran was not legally required to implement.

U.N. Charter and the Security Council

Several articles of the U.N. Charter, which is a treaty, describe the Security Council's authority to impose requirements and sanctions on Iran.[37] Article 24 confers on the council "primary responsibility for the maintenance of international peace and security." The article also states that the "specific powers granted to the Security Council for the discharge of these duties are laid down" in several chapters of the charter, including Chapter VII, which describes the actions that the council may take in response to "threats to the peace, breaches of the peace, and acts of aggression."

Chapter VII of the charter contains three articles relevant to the Iran case. Security Council resolutions that made mandatory the IAEA's demands concerning Iran's nuclear program invoked Chapter VII. Article 39 of that chapter states that the council

> shall determine the existence of any threat to the peace, breach of the peace, or act of aggression and shall make recommendations, or decide what measures shall be taken in accordance with Articles 41 and 42, to maintain or restore international peace and security.

Resolution 1696 invoked Article 40 of Chapter VII "in order to make mandatory the suspension required by the IAEA." As noted, that resolution did not impose any sanctions on Iran. Article 40 states that

> the Security Council may, before making the recommendations or deciding upon the measures provided for in Article 39 [of Chapter VII], call upon the parties concerned to comply with such provisional measures as it deems necessary or desirable.

Resolutions 1737, 1747, 1803, and 1929, which did impose sanctions, invoked Article 41 of Chapter VII. According to Article 41, the Security Council

> may decide what measures not involving the use of armed force are to be employed to give effect to its decisions, and it may call upon the Members of the United Nations to apply such measures. These may include complete or partial interruption of economic relations and of rail, sea, air, postal, telegraphic, radio, and other means of communication, and the severance of diplomatic relations.

As noted, Security Council resolution 1835 did not impose new sanctions, but reaffirmed the previous resolutions and called on Iran to comply with them.

It is worth noting that Article 25 of the U.N. Charter obligates U.N. members "to accept and carry out the decisions of the Security Council."

---

[37] The text of the charter is available at http://www.un.org/aboutun/charter/.

Has Iran Violated the NPT?[38]

Whether Iran has violated the NPT is unclear. The treaty does not contain a mechanism for determining that a state-party has violated its obligations. Moreover, there does not appear to be a formal procedure for determining such violations. An NPT Review Conference would, however, be one venue for NPT states-parties to make such a determination.

The U.N. Security Council has never declared Iran to be in violation of the NPT; neither the council nor the U.N. General Assembly has a responsibility to adjudicate treaty violations. However, the lack of a ruling by the council on Iran's compliance with the NPT has apparently had little practical effect because, as noted, the council has taken action in response to the IAEA Board of Governors' determination that Iran has violated its safeguards agreement.

Iran's violations of its safeguards agreement appear to constitute violations of Article III, which requires NPT non-nuclear-weapon states-parties to accept IAEA safeguards, in accordance with the agency's statue, "for the exclusive purpose of verification of the fulfillment of its obligations assumed under this Treaty with a view to preventing diversion of nuclear energy from peaceful uses to nuclear weapons or other nuclear explosive devices."

Tehran may also have violated provisions of Article II which state that non-nuclear-weapon states-parties shall not "manufacture or otherwise acquire nuclear weapons or other nuclear explosive devices" or "seek or receive any assistance in the manufacture of nuclear weapons or other nuclear explosive devices."

As noted, the IAEA is continuing to investigate evidence of what ElBaradei described in June 2008 as "possible military dimensions to Iran's nuclear programme." [39] Such activities may indicate that Tehran has violated both Article II provisions described above. Moreover, a November 2007 National Intelligence Estimate (NIE) stated that "until fall 2003, Iranian military entities were working under government direction to develop nuclear weapons." This past program could be a violation of Article II, although the estimate does not provide any detail about the program. Nevertheless, the IAEA has never reported that Iran has attempted to develop nuclear weapons.

Despite the lack of such an IAEA conclusion, a 2005 State Department report regarding states' compliance with nonproliferation agreements argued that the country had violated Article II of the NPT:

> The breadth of Iran's nuclear development efforts, the secrecy and deceptions with which they have been conducted for nearly 20 years, its redundant and surreptitious procurement channels, Iran's persistent failure to comply with its obligations to report to the IAEA and to apply safeguards to such activities, and the lack of a reasonable economic justification for this program leads us to conclude that Iran is pursuing an effort to manufacture nuclear weapons, and has sought and received assistance in this effort in violation of Article II of the NPT.[40]

---

[38] Portions of this section are based on interviews with U.N. and State Department officials.

[39] Available at http://www.dni.gov/press_releases/20071203_release.pdf.

[40] *Adherence to and Compliance with Arms Control, Nonproliferation and Disarmament Agreements and Commitments*, Department of State, August 2005, available at http://www.state.gov/documents/organization/52113.pdf.

The report also stated that Iran's "weapons program combines elements" of Tehran's declared nuclear activities, as well as suspected "undeclared fuel cycle and other activities that may exist, including those that may be run solely be the military."

The State Department's reasoning appears to be based on an interpretation of the NPT which holds that a wide scope of nuclear activities could constitute violations of Article II. The 2005 report states that assessments regarding Article II compliance "must look at the totality of the facts, including judgments as to" a state-party's "purpose in undertaking the nuclear activities in question." The report also includes a list of activities which could constitute such non-compliance.[41]

The 2005 State Department report cites testimony from then-Arms Control and Disarmament Agency Director William Foster during a 1968 Senate Foreign Relations Committee hearing.[42] Foster stated that "facts indicating that the purpose of a particular activity was the acquisition of a nuclear explosive device would tend to show non-compliance" with Article II. He gave two examples: "the construction of an experimental or prototype nuclear explosive device" and "the production of components which could only have relevance" to such a device. However, Foster also noted that a variety of other activities could also violate Article II, adding that the United States believed it impossible "to formulate a comprehensive definition or interpretation."

It is worth noting that the 2005 State Department report's arguments appear to rely heavily on the notion that a state's apparent intentions underlying certain nuclear-related activities can be used to determine violations of Article II. This interpretation is not shared by all experts.[43]

The 2005 report "primarily reflected activities from January 2002 through December 2003." Whether the State Department assesses that Iran has violated Article II since then is unclear. A version of the report released in 2010, which "primarily reflect[s] activities from January 1, 2004, through December 31, 2008," states that "the issues underlying" the 2005 report's conclusion regarding Iran's Article II compliance "remain unresolved."[44] The 2011 version of the report, which "primarily reflect[s] activities from January 1, 2009, through December 31, 2010," reiterates the 2010 report's assessment.[45] As noted, the 2007 NIE assessed that Iran halted its nuclear weapons program in 2003.

---

[41] According to the report, such activities can include (1) the presence of undeclared nuclear facilities; (2) procurement patterns inconsistent with a civil nuclear program (e.g., clandestine procurement networks, possibly including the use of front companies, false end-use information, and fraudulent documentation); (3) security measures beyond what would be appropriate for peaceful, civil nuclear installations; (4) a pattern of Article III safeguards violations suggestive not of mere mistake or incompetence, but of willful violation and/or systematic deception and denial efforts aimed at concealing nuclear activities from the IAEA; and (5) a nuclear program with little (or no) coherence for peaceful purposes, but great coherence for weapons purposes.

[42] *Nonproliferation Treaty*, Senate Committee on Foreign Relations, Joint Committee on Atomic Energy [Part 1] July 10-12, 17, 1968; Session 90-2 (1968). The complete statement regarding Article II violations is in **Appendix B**.

[43] Personal communication with Andreas Persbo, Senior Researcher, the Verification Research, Training and Information Centre.

[44] Quotations are from *Adherence to and Compliance with Arms Control, Nonproliferation, and Disarmament Agreements and Commitments*, Department of State, July 2010, available at http://www.state.gov/t/avc/rls/rpt/c9721 htm.

[45] Adherence to and Compliance with Arms Control, Nonproliferation, and Disarmament Agreements and Commitments, Department of State, August 2011, available at http://www.state.gov/t/avc/rls/rpt/c9721 htm.

Appendix A. Iranian Noncompliance with Its IAEA Safeguards Agreement

The November 2003 report (GOV/2003/75) from IAEA Director-General ElBaradei to the agency's Board of Governors details what the September 2005 board resolution described as "Iran's many failures and breaches of its obligations to comply with its safeguards agreement."

The report stated that

> Iran has failed in a number of instances over an extended period of time to meet its obligations under its Safeguards Agreement with respect to the reporting of nuclear material and its processing and use, as well as the declaration of facilities where such material has been processed and stored.

The report detailed some of these failures and referenced other failures described in two earlier reports (GOV/2003/40 and GOV/2003/63) from ElBaradei to the IAEA board.[46]

According to GOV/2003/40, Iran failed to declare the following activities to the agency:

- The importation of natural uranium, and its subsequent transfer for further processing.

- The processing and use of the imported natural uranium, including the production and loss of nuclear material, and the production and transfer of resulting waste.

Additionally, Iran failed to

- declare the facilities where nuclear material (including the waste) was received, stored and processed,

- provide in a timely manner updated design information for a research reactor located in Tehran, as well as

- provide in a timely manner information on two waste storage sites.

GOV/2003/63 stated that Iran failed to report uranium conversion experiments to the IAEA. According to GOV/2003/75, Iran failed to report the following activities to the IAEA:

- The use of imported natural uranium hexafluoride for the testing of centrifuges, as well as the subsequent production of enriched and depleted uranium.

- The importation of natural uranium metal and its subsequent transfer for use in laser enrichment experiments, including the production of enriched uranium, the loss of nuclear material during these operations, and the production and transfer of resulting waste.

- The production of a variety of nuclear compounds from several different imported nuclear materials, and the production and transfer of resulting wastes.

---

[46] Those reports are available at http://www.iaea.org/Publications/Documents/Board/2003/gov2003-40.pdf and http://www.iaea.org/Publications/Documents/Board/2003/gov2003-63.pdf.

- The production of uranium targets and their irradiation in the Tehran Research Reactor, the subsequent processing of those targets (including the separation of plutonium), the production and transfer of resulting waste, and the storage of unprocessed irradiated targets.

Iran also failed to provide the agency with design information for a variety of nuclear-related facilities, according to the report. These included the following:

- A centrifuge testing facility.

- Two laser laboratories and locations where resulting wastes were processed.

- Facilities involved in the production of a variety of nuclear compounds.

- The Tehran Research Reactor (with respect to the irradiation of uranium targets), the hot cell facility where the plutonium separation took place, as well as the relevant waste handling facility.

Additionally, the report cited Iran's "failure on many occasions to co-operate to facilitate the implementation of safeguards, through concealment" of its nuclear activities.

Appendix B. Extended Remarks by William Foster Regarding Possible NPT Article II Violations

On July 10, 1968, then-Arms Control and Disarmament Agency Director William Foster testified before the Senate Foreign Relations Committee about the NPT. In response to a question regarding the type of nuclear activities prohibited by Article II of the treaty, Foster supplied the following statement:

> Extension of Remarks by Mr. Foster in Response to Question Regarding Nuclear Explosive Devices
>
> The treaty articles in question are Article II, in which non-nuclear-weapon parties undertake 'not to manufacture or otherwise acquire nuclear weapons or other nuclear explosive devices,' and Article IV, which provides that nothing in the Treaty is to be interpreted as affecting the right of all Parties to the Treaty 'to develop research, production and use of nuclear energy for peaceful purposes…in conformity with Articles I and II of this Treaty.' In the course of the negotiation of the Treaty, United States representatives were asked their views on what would constitute the 'manufacture' of a nuclear weapon or other nuclear explosive device under Article II of the draft treaty. Our reply was as follows:
>
> 'While the general intent of this provision seems clear, and its application to cases such as those discussed below should present little difficulty, the United States believe [sic] it is not possible at this time to formulate a comprehensive definition or interpretation. There are many hypothetical situations which might be imagined and it is doubtful that any general definition or interpretation, unrelated to specific fact situations could satisfactorily deal with all such situations.
>
> 'Some general observations can be made with respect to the question of whether or not a specific activity constitutes prohibited manufacture under the proposed treaty. For example, facts indicating that the purpose of a particular activity was the acquisition of a nuclear explosive device would tend to show non-compliance. (Thus, the construction of an experimental or prototype nuclear explosive device would be covered by the term 'manufacture' as would be the production of components which could only have relevance to a nuclear explosive device.) Again, while the placing of a particular activity under safeguards would not, in and of itself, settle the question of whether that activity was in compliance with the treaty, it would of course be helpful in allaying any suspicion of non-compliance.
>
> 'It may be useful to point out, for illustrative purposes, several activities which the United States would not consider per se to be violations of the prohibitions in Article II. Neither uranium enrichment nor the stockpiling of fissionable material in connection with a peaceful program would violate Article II so long as these activities were safeguarded under Article III. Also clearly permitted would be the development, under safeguards, of plutonium fueled power reactors, including research on the properties of metallic plutonium, nor would Article II interfere with the development or use of fast breeder reactors under safeguards.'

Author Contact Information

Paul K. Kerr
Analyst in Nonproliferation
pkerr@crs.loc.gov, 7-8693